A LOOK AT ANTS

A LOOK AT ANTS

ROSS E. HUTCHINS

With photographs by the author

DODD, MEAD & COMPANY / New York

Frontispiece: Close-up of a leaf-cutting ant.

1 2 3 4 5 6 7 8 9 10

Library of Congress Cataloging in Publication Data

Hutchins, Ross E
   A look at ants.

   SUMMARY: Describes the physical characteristics,
habits, and natural environment of various kinds of
ants.
   1. Ants—Juvenile literature. [1. Ants] I. Title.
QL568.F7H843   595.7′96   77–16867
ISBN 0–396–07539–8

Contents

Ants' eyes, like most insect eyes, are made up of hundreds of tiny simple eyes. This close-up is the eye of an Australian bulldog ant.

Some ants have brushes on their front legs. They use them to clean their antennae, or feelers.

What Is an Ant?

You have no doubt seen an ant. They are common insects, like butterflies, moths, beetles, and bees. All these insects have certain characteristics. Their bodies are divided into three parts: *head, thorax,* and *abdomen.* Located on the head are the antennae (or feelers), the mouthparts, and the eyes. Each large eye is made up of hundreds of tiny, simple eyes.

To the thorax, or middle section, are attached three pairs of legs and, in many cases, one or two pairs of wings. The rear end, or abdomen, contains digestive and reproductive organs. Some insects have stings.

Insects' muscles and other organs are enclosed in hard shells. Their shell-like bodies are joined in several places to allow movement. This is also true of their legs. That is the reason they are classified as Arthropods, meaning "joint-footed."

All insects have a head, thorax, and abdomen. Ants have another small segment between the thorax and abdomen. You can see it clearly in this large ant (Dinoponera) *from Brazil.*

Ants belong to a special family of insects, the Formicidae. If you look closely at an ant, you can see a tiny, extra segment between the thorax and abdomen. This extra segment is peculiar to ants. Ants also have large jaws which they use for almost everything—for capturing other insects, cutting up seeds, digging in the ground, making tunnels in wood.

Most ants are black or brown. One kind, found in the Tropics, is green. Worker ants range in size from very tiny to over an inch long. Certain winged queen ants are larger, some as much as two inches long. Many ants have stings. They have keen vision, but a few kinds are blind.

Harvester ants like this one use their powerful jaws to cut up seeds.

Ants use their jaws for almost everything. This bulldog ant uses its pincerlike jaws to capture insect "game."

The jaws of this leaf-cutting ant are used to cut sections out of leaves.

There are about 8,000 different kinds of ants, and they live in almost all parts of the world except the coldest regions.

THE LIVES OF ANTS

Ants are *social* insects. This means that they live together in colonies that sometimes contain thousands of individual ants. One red ant colony, for example, had 238,000 members.

In a typical ant colony there are usually three kinds of individuals. These are the queen, many worker ants, and a few males. Sometimes there are also soldier ants. The queen is the only one that can mate and lay eggs. The ant world is a world of females. All the worker and soldier ants are females, though they do not mate or lay eggs.

Males are present only at certain periods of the year. It is at

Ants often communicate, or exchange messages, by touching antennae, or feelers. These are carpenter ants that nest in wood.

Queen ants have wings, but their wings are shed after mating.

this time that new queens are produced and when "swarming" occurs. During swarming the new queens and the males leave the nest. The queens mate and fly away to start new ant colonies. The males die. Once the new queen has started her own colony, she sheds her wings. She will have no further use for them.

Only the queens and males have wings. All the workers and soldiers are wingless. Worker ants are the ones usually seen crawling about when a nest is disturbed. They do all the work of nest building, gathering food, and caring for the young.

During its development, an ant passes through four steps, or stages. This is called its *life history*. These steps are the egg, grub (*larva*), resting stage (*pupa*), and adult ant. During the larval stage the ant is blind and has no legs. It is fed and cared for by the worker ants. When fully developed, the larva (plural, *larvae*) sheds its skin and changes into a pupa (plural, *pupae*). Pupal ants do not feed, and may or may not be enclosed in cocoons. After a certain period, the pupal ants shed their skins for the last time and the adult ants emerge. The time from egg to adult usually takes about three months.

As a general rule, worker ants have very short lives. They live only a few weeks or months. Queens live much longer, sometimes for five or six years, and continue to lay eggs.

Ants of one kind or another live in almost every type of habitat, or place, you can imagine. Many ants make their nests under

Ant workers feed and care for the young. Here two black carpenter ants are carrying one of the larvae.

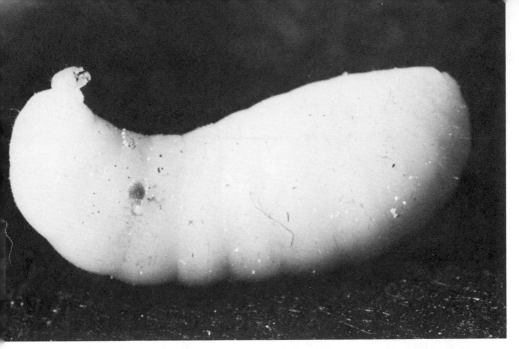

Ant larvae, or young, are white and grub-like. They are fed and cared for by the worker ants.

When fully developed, ant larvae change into pupae. During this stage they are helpless and do not eat. Later, they change into adult ants.

stones. Others live in rotten logs or under the bark of dead trees. There are several kinds of ants that make their nests in the hollow stems of plants and trees. Some build nests by fastening leaves together with silk.

The food habits of ants are as varied as the places where they live. Some feed on seeds. Others capture and eat other insects. Several kinds gather the sweet sap of plants, while others protect aphids or plant lice for the sweet honeydew they produce.

Unfortunately for us, ants of several kinds are pests in our homes where they destroy foods or damage products. Other ants are harmful to crops or gardens. A number of ants—like the imported fire ant of the Southeast—have stings that are harmful to people.

Many kinds of ants have stings, like bees. This is a stinging ant from the South Pacific islands.

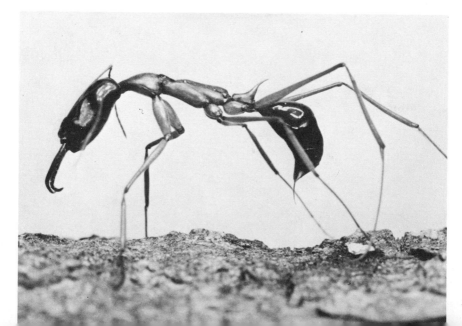

Bulldog ants live in tunnels in the ground. They will rush out and attack enemies.

THE WARRIORS AND HUNTERS

Many ants live by hunting and eating insects and other small creatures. Among the most vicious of the hunting ants are the bulldog ants (*Myrmecia*) that live in the eucalyptus forests of Australia. These ants are nearly an inch long and have large, toothed jaws. They also have stings that may cause great pain. These savage ants will rush out of their underground tunnels and attack any intruder. They can kill an insect as large as a huge beetle. Some can jump more than a foot, an unusual habit for an ant.

15

Common in many parts of the United States are red wood ants (*Formica*) that build mounds of small twigs and pine needles. These ants are hunters, too. But since some of the insects they capture and eat are pests of gardens, these ants are beneficial to us. One *myrmecologist* (a student of ants) observed that a colony of these ants brought in twenty-eight dead insects in a minute. He estimated that this colony of ants captured about 10,000 insects a day.

Probably the world's most dangerous hunting ants are the army ants (*Eciton*) in the jungles of Central and South America, and the driver ants (*Dorylus*) found in Africa. Strange to say, both kinds are blind. Only the winged males have eyes.

Army ants stream through the jungle in large numbers. Usually the marching columns are about five ants wide. They

Army ants march through the jungles in search of insect "game." These are the large-jawed soldiers and a smaller worker ant (center).

Army ant soldiers have large jaws shaped like ice tongs. Their duty is to defend the colony from enemies.

travel at the rate of a hundred feet an hour. Army ants have no real homes or nests. A colony moves through the jungle for seventeen days, stopping each night, then moving on again. At the end of the seventeen-day period they stop and establish a temporary nest while the huge queen produces nearly 30,000 eggs. During this time the ants make daily raids into the surrounding area in search of "game." This is carried back to the nest. At the end of twenty days the eggs hatch and the ants begin moving through the jungle again, carrying the young, grub-like ants with them. Now they travel at night and search for "game" during the day.

Close-up of an army worker ant carrying a pincer from a scorpion. Army ants can carry heavy weights.

By the end of twenty days the larval ants are ready to spin cocoons, so the ants settle down in another temporary nest and remain there until the young ants come out of their cocoons and are able to travel. In this way these ants continue their nomadic habits for month after month and year after year. Always, when marching to new locations, the ants all travel in one direction. The strong-jawed soldiers are on guard along the sides of the moving column.

Closely related to the army ants are the driver ants of South Africa. These ants have habits quite similar to the army ants, but are even more vicious. They will attack almost any animal, no matter how large it is. A full-grown leopard, confined in a cage, was once killed and eaten in one night by driver ants.

Driver ant workers are small, only one-eighth to a quarter of an inch in length. The large-jawed soldiers are much larger, nearly half an inch long. The winged queens resemble wasps and are nearly two inches long.

Like honeybees, driver ants send out scouts looking for "game." When food is located, the rest of the ants hurry to the attack. Army ants do not send out scouts.

Both army and driver ants are like human armies on the march. They travel across the land, obtaining their food as they go. They have no fixed homes.

A marching column of African driver ants. The workers walk in the center with the soldiers on guard along the sides.

Driver ant soldiers have large jaws but, like the workers, they are blind. Only the winged males have eyes.

A queen driver ant is much larger than the workers or soldiers, nearly two inches long. Only the queens and males have wings.

Most of the ants we see on picnics make their nests in the ground or under stones. But there are many ants that live in trees or in rotten wood. Common in most places are the large, black carpenter ants (*Camponotus*), often seen hurrying about in forested areas. They are called carpenter ants because they make their nests in rotten logs, using their sharp jaws to cut away the wood. They may even cut tunnels in very hard wood. They feed on small insects captured in the area. These are carried back into the nest.

Other kinds of ants live in or on trees. Many of these are found in tropical lands, but a few occur here in our own country. One kind is the *Colobopsis* ant that makes tunnels in the twigs of white ash, sumac, or other trees that have twigs filled with soft pith. These ants must, of course, have a way of getting into the twigs. So they cut round holes in them.

In a *Colobopsis* nest there are workers, a queen, and a few soldiers. (At certain seasons a few winged males may be present.) The soldier ants are the most unusual. They have large, plug-shaped heads which they use like stoppers to close the round entrances to the nest tunnel. This keeps out strange ants and other enemies. At all times, one of these soldiers keeps its head in the entrance hole. The food of these ants consists of

Colobopsis *ants live inside twigs. This twig has been cut open to show a soldier ant with its plug-shaped head.*

This is how the soldier uses its head like a stopper to plug the entrance hole of the nest tunnel. The worker ant (bottom) does not have a plug-shaped head.

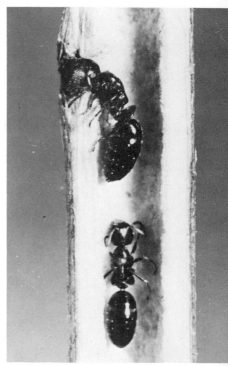

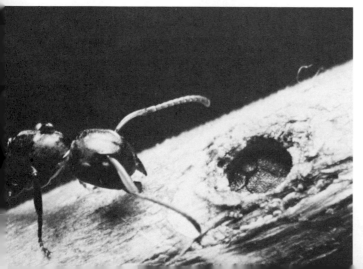

To enter the entrance hole, this Colobopsis *worker ant must first give the "password" by touching the soldier's head.*

honeydew gathered from plant lice that live on the leaves of the tree. When a worker ant returns to the nest with honeydew, it taps on the soldier's head in a certain way. This is the "password" and the soldier backs away and allows the worker to enter. After the worker has gone into the nest, the soldier again closes the hole with its head.

In Mexico there are acacia trees that furnish ants with both food and shelter. The trees have large, hollow thorns that grow in pairs. The thorns look like bulls' horns, so the plant is called the bull-horn acacia. There are ants (*Pseudomyrma*) that make snug homes inside these hollow thorns. The ants make small entrance holes near the end of one pair of thorns. Growing near the base of each leaf is a row of *nectaries* that produce a sweet

Pseudomyrma ants live inside these bull-horn acacia thorns. Notice the ants' entrance hole in the left thorn.

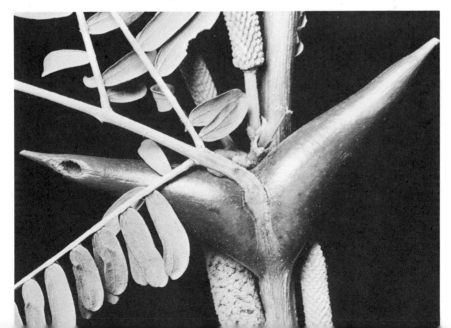

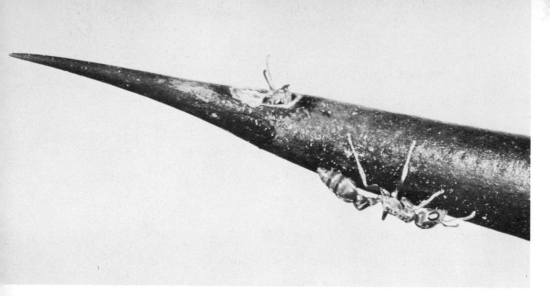

An ant peeks out of the entrance to its nest inside an acacia thorn. Another worker ant poses on the outside of the thorn.

sap or honeydew upon which the ants feed. Other food for the ants are tiny fruit-like growths at the tips of the leaflets. These are eagerly gathered by the ants.

Now you may wonder why the acacia tree goes to all this trouble. The answer is simple. The ants living in the thorns crawl about over the tree searching for food. As they do, they drive away any leaf-eating insects they find. This protects the acacia tree. The tree helps the ants and, in return, the ants help the tree. This is an example of plant-animal cooperation called *symbiosis*. This is where two living things live together for mutual benefit.

Other unusual tree-dwelling ants are the weaver ants (*Oeco-*

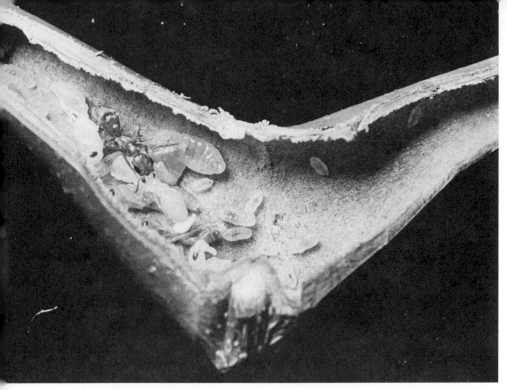

Here a pair of acacia thorns has been cut open to show the ant colony inside. Present are pupae and larvae.

A close-up of the nectaries that produce food for the ants.

phylla). One kind lives in Ceylon and another in Brazil. These ants fasten leaves together to make leaf-nests. The ants live inside these nests, protected from weather and enemies. They build the nests by "sewing" the leaves together with silk.

What is so unusual about the weaver ants is their source of silk. Adult worker ants do not have silk glands and so cannot produce silk. But these ants have solved the problem. Their young, or larvae, *do* have silk glands. The adult ants grasp their larvae in their jaws and, using them like bobbins, "sew" the edges of the leaves together. When the silk hardens, the leaves are held together very securely.

The Mushroom Growers

Ants have many "trades" or ways of making a living. Most amazing is the fact that many of their ways are quite similar to our own. We have already seen that there are hunting and weaver ants. But would you expect ant farmers? Some ants actually grow crops as a source of food. The crops they cultivate are mushrooms or fungi. Such ants are found here in the United States, as well as in some tropical lands.

In the eastern United States dwell at least two kinds of fungus-growing ants. One is *Trachymyrmex*, small ants that we might call the "little" leaf-cutters.

26

Left: Trachymyrmex *leaf-cutters working in their underground fungus garden. Right: The nest cavity of the little leaf-cutters is about the size of an orange. Notice the masses of growing fungus.*

These little ants make their nests underground in sandy soil. The entrance to such a nest is a small hole. If you were to dig downward, you would find a round cavity about six inches below the surface. This cavity, about the size of an orange, would be filled with a gray, spongy mass of fungus. It is upon this fungus that the ants feed.

In order to nourish this fungus, the ants gather bits of plant material or caterpillar droppings and carry them into the nest. Sometimes they cut small sections out of leaves or from the

Leaf-cutting ants carry pieces of leaves to their underground nest.

petals of flowers. I once kept a colony of these ants in my studio for more than a year by supplying the ants with chopped-up rose petals.

Of all the fungus-growing ants, the large leaf-cutters (*Atta*) are the most amazing. These ants range from southern Louisiana and Texas down into Central and South America. I studied and photographed them in a deep forest in Louisiana. It was near midnight when my wife and I came upon the ants. Suddenly we saw a long column of ants hurrying down a trail about two inches wide. Each worker was carrying a piece of leaf about the size of a dime. The ants held the leaf fragments over their heads.

Going on for several hundred feet, we saw the ants carrying

28

the leaves into a hole in the ground. The hole was about an inch in diameter.

The next morning we returned and began digging into the sandy soil. A few feet below the surface we found several of the ants' nest cavities. Each one was about the size of a watermelon and was filled with a mass of gray fungus. We could see many ants of various sizes. Some were busy cutting up the leaves that had been carried into the nest the night before. The bits were being placed in the growing fungus to nourish it. Also present were many tiny ants. These were the "weeders" whose work was removing unwanted molds from the fungus.

The fungus grown by the *Atta* ants is actually the underground stage of a mushroom. If one of these fungus gardens is abandoned by the ants, it will grow into a mushroom.

At certain seasons, usually from April to July, winged males and queens swarm out of the underground nests. Before leaving, each queen fills her mouth with a bit of fungus. After mating, she digs a small tunnel in the ground and spits out the bit of fungus she has brought with her. This will, in time, develop into a fungus garden for her and her new ant colony. This is the way that a new *Atta* ant colony is started.

The leaf-cutting ants often cause great damage to trees and gardens. A large tree may have all its leaves cut off and carried away in a single night by these "mushroom growers."

Close-up of an Atta ant holding a piece it has cut out of a leaf. These ants can carry heavy loads.

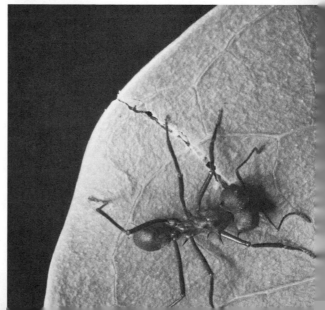

A leaf-cutting ant snipping out a section of a tree leaf. It uses its sharp jaws like scissors.

THE HONEY GATHERERS

Many ants gather nectar and honeydew from plants and flowers. In return for this food, the ants drive away leaf-eating enemies that might harm the plants.

Of the many kinds of sweet-eating ants, the honey ants (*Myrmecocystus*) of southwestern United States are the most unusual. One of the best places to observe and study these ants is in the Garden of the Gods near Colorado Springs, Colorado. There I found the entrances to their underground nests along the sandy ridges. Nearby were scrub oaks with marble-like growths on their twigs. These, I knew, had been produced by tiny wasps that lived inside them. These growths are called *galls*, and their outer surfaces are covered with sweet honeydew. The honey ants gather this substance at night.

I returned after dark to watch the ants and to take pictures of

Galls like this one on a scrub oak produce honeydew. It is gathered by the worker ants and carried back to the nest.

them. With a flashlight I watched the honey ants coming out of their tunnels and crawling up the oaks where they filled themselves with honeydew from the galls.

Early the next morning I dug down into the hard ground beside one of the ant mounds. Several inches below the surface I came to one of the underground chambers. It was a little more than an inch high and about six inches across. From the ceiling hung many ants with their abdomens swollen to the size of small grapes. They were so full they were nearly helpless. Several had fallen to the floor where they lay, waving their legs in the air. They were so heavy with honeydew that they could not climb back up to the ceiling. One or two had burst. I tasted the honey-

Honey ants in their underground chamber, with several repletes hanging from the ceiling, and some normal worker ants.

The abdomen of this honey ant replete is swollen with honeydew.

dew, and it reminded me of sugar syrup. The local Indians once gathered these ants as a source of sweets.

The ants with their abdomens swollen with honeydew are called *repletes*. They serve out their entire lives as "storage tanks" for the honeydew gathered by the other workers from the oak galls. Once they have taken on the job of storage tanks, the repletes never leave the nest chamber again. They are the ants' only method of storing the liquid food upon which they live. When a worker ant is hungry, it taps on the head of a replete, who spits up a droplet of honeydew.

These honey ants have adapted to life in a barren land where food can be gathered only during a short period of each year. They have solved the storage problem in a unique way.

The Herdsmen

Early man tamed wild cattle and goats for their milk. Ants, too, keep "livestock" as a source of food. This livestock consists of aphids, or plant lice, that produce sweet honeydew upon which the ants feed. In return, the ants protect their aphid "cattle" from enemies such as beetles.

Aphids suck out the sap of plants. They are very helpless and have many enemies. Each aphid has two horn-like tubes attached to the rear end of its body. From these tubes the aphid releases droplets of honeydew that ants like to eat. If a beetle attacks one of the aphid "cows," the ants drive it away, thus saving the aphid from harm.

Some kinds of aphids cannot get along without their ant friends. They are never found without them. One kind, known

Aphids (here, much enlarged) suck out the sap of plants. Ants feed on the honeydew they release.

as the cornfield aphid, lives on the roots of corn and is completely dependent upon certain ants. In autumn, the ants carry the aphids' eggs into underground nests where they are kept all winter. When spring comes, the ants carry the eggs out and place them on the stems of the corn plants where they hatch and produce "herds" of aphid "cows." These aphids have been living with the ants for so long that they cannot do without their help.

Some kinds of ants build "barns" for their livestock. One example is the acrobatic ant. These ants construct shelters for their aphids by surrounding twigs with "roofs" of plant fibers

35

Some ants build "barns" for their aphid livestock. This one was made of plant fibers cemented together. Note the ant entering the nest.

Here the roof of an ant "barn" has been removed. These "cows" are mealybugs which, like aphids, also produce honeydew.

cemented together. Inside these shelters the aphids live, protected from weather and enemies. These ants also keep mealybugs and the caterpillars of little blue butterflies as sources of honeydew.

Probably the most remarkable instance of ants caring for butterfly caterpillars is found in southern Mexico. The ants are a kind of carpenter ant (*Camponotus*) that make their nests in trees and plants. During the day, the caterpillars are kept in holes or "pens" at the bases of croton plants. Just before dusk, the ants go up and explore the leaves of the plant to make sure that no enemies are present. If all is well, the little caterpillars

Ants and their "herds" of aphid "cows" on a leaf.

are allowed to crawl up the plants and out onto the leaves where they can feed. Just before dawn the ants herd their caterpillars down the stem and into their "pens." They are kept there all day, safe from most enemies.

THE GRAIN HARVESTERS

If you have ever traveled across the Western plains you have probably noticed large, mound-shaped ant hills surrounded by bare, sandy areas. These are the homes of harvester ants (*Pogonomyrmex*) that gather and store seeds.

If you should examine one of these ant hills you would find piles of seed hulls around the outer edges of the surrounding cleared space. These hulls were discarded by the ants after they had removed the seeds. It is the seeds that the ants eat.

Inside the ant hill you would find many chambers and tunnels. Some of the chambers would be filled with seeds, while others would contain young ants. The seed-filled chambers are the ants' grain bins.

During daylight hours the ants go out to gather seeds. These are carried back into the nest where the hulls are cut off and carried out and discarded along the edges of the cleared space around the ant hill.

The ant hill chambers are all connected by passages. Those

near the top are used for rearing young. Deeper in the ground are chambers where the ants spend the winter. These may be many feet below the level of the ground. One harvester colony in Arizona had 436 chambers. The lowest ones were about fifteen feet below the surface. This ant colony contained 12,358 ants. Harvester ants can sting painfully, as I quickly found out when I began studying them.

Inside the ant colony there is a division of labor or duties. Deep within the nest is the royal chamber where the queen lives and lays her eggs. After the eggs hatch, the young ants, or larvae, are taken up to the higher chambers where they are fed and cared for by the worker ants.

Deeper down are chambers for seed storage. Here, in total darkness, the ants toil at the work of removing the husks and

Harvester ants build two-foot high mounds. Inside are many passages and chambers. (See next photograph.)

Some of the passages and chambers inside a harvester ant hill contain young ants. Others are used as grain bins for seed storage.

cutting up the seeds that have been carried into the nest.

As you might guess, the seeds stored in the underground chambers often sprout, especially during rainy periods. Thus, it becomes necessary for the ants to carry the seeds out of the nest and dry them in the sun.

Harvester ants of some kinds have large-headed workers with powerful jaws. It is believed that these workers use their jaws to cut up the hard seeds so that they can be eaten.

In digging their tunnels and chambers, it is not unusual for the ants to find pebbles. These must be removed. I once saw one of these ants lifting a large pebble out of its nest entrance. I captured the ant and weighed it and the pebble. The pebble weighed more than fifty times as much as the ant. This is equal to a man lifting nearly four tons!

The ants often have more than a quart of seeds in their bins. As might be expected, prairie rats and mice frequently dig into the nests and carry off the stored food.

A harvester ant cares for young ants (pupae) in one of the chambers.

A harvester ant carries a seed into its underground nest.

Harvester ants can lift and carry heavy loads. This pebble weighed 52 times as much as the ant.

This little cricket (left) lives happily with black carpenter ants.

Ant Guests and "Spongers"

Since ants are social insects and live in nests where there is both food and shelter, it is not surprising that a number of "guest" insects move in with them. There are many of these ant guests. They are called *myrmecophiles*, meaning "ant-loving." Tiny crickets, cockroaches, beetles, fly larvae, and some spiders live with ants.

The little cockroaches that dwell with the leaf-cutting ants are blind. After taking up life with the ants, millions of years ago, they lived in the darkness of underground tunnels where they had no need for eyes. Their eyes disappeared.

Some of these guests feed on food brought into the ants' nests, while others lick off the oil on the ants' bodies. This would seem

43

Tiny crickets live with harvester ants. Here one of these "guests" licks the hind leg of a worker ant.

to be dangerous, but the guests always seem able to avoid the jaws of their hosts.

Most ants merely put up with their guests. But some guests appear to be kept by the ants for the secretions they produce and on which the ants feed. One of these is a small scarab beetle that is actually held captive by the ants. If one of these beetles tries to leave the ant nest, it is carried back inside.

There is a family of ant-loving beetles that have small clumps of hairs on their bodies. When an ant touches one of these clumps, a sweetish liquid is released. The ants are very fond of this and lap it up. The sad truth is that this beetle liquid is, to the ants, almost like a drug. One kind of these little beetles lives with black carpenter ants. The ants like them so much that they neglect their own young, which become undernourished. Not

44

only do the ants care for these strange guests, but the guests often eat the young ants.

THE SLAVE KEEPERS

In Africa there are some ants with evil habits. In order to start a new colony the queen flies down to the nest of another kind of ant called *Tapinoma* where she is dragged inside. Very foolishly, these ants do not kill her. After awhile this evil queen cuts off the head of the *Tapinoma* queen and starts laying her own eggs in the nest. The strange thing is that the workers care for the young that hatch from these eggs just as if they were their own sisters, hatched from eggs laid by their own queen.

In time, the *Tapinoma* workers all die off and the nest becomes populated entirely with the evil queen's workers. Because of the queen's habit of cutting off the head of the *Tapinoma* queen, these ants are known as "beheading" ants.

While we consider most ants to be industrious, there are a few kinds that are not so deserving. Some ants make slaves of other ants, forcing them to do their work. A common mound-building ant, the red *Formica*, makes slaves of black *Formicas*.

The red *Formicas* are actually kidnappers. Several times a year they make raids on nests of black *Formicas* and carry off their young, both larvae and pupae. These are taken back to the

A vicious red Formica *ant (left) with one of its black* Formica *slaves.*

red *Formica* nest where a few of them are eaten and the rest allowed to develop into adult ants. These new workers aid their kidnappers in carrying out all the work of the colony. Sometimes they even go out on slave-catching raids with their masters.

ANT ENEMIES

In the animal world there are those that are hardworking and those that are lazy. As we have seen, harvester ants gather and store large amounts of grain or seeds. But thieves sometimes steal the harvester ants' grain. The yellow thief ant (*Solenopsis*) builds its nest near harvester nests. These little ants make tunnels into those of the harvesters. Since the tunnels of the thief

46

ants are very small, the larger harvester ants cannot follow them. The thief ants are left alone to rob the harvesters' grain bins whenever they wish.

Another seed-eating ant (*Dorymyrmex*) makes its nest near harvester nests. These ants steal food the harvester ants may be carrying home. They also go into their nests and take their grain.

Ants also have other enemies that kill and eat them. Birds of many kinds prey on them. In the West, horned toads lie in wait and gobble up any ant that passes by. Ordinary frogs and toads also capture and eat ants.

Among the most interesting of the ant enemies are ant-lions.

Horned toads often lie in wait and capture harvester ants while they are out hunting for seeds.

Ant-lions are the young, or larval stage, of winged insects. They have large, sharp jaws and dig pits in the sand. When an ant walks by, it is apt to tumble into the pit and roll down into the bottom. Then it is grabbed by the ant-lion and eaten.

Larval tiger beetles also capture ants. They are slender and look like caterpillars. They are often called "doodlebugs." They dig pencil-sized holes several inches deep in the ground. The doodlebug rests in the hole with only its head and jaws above the ground. When an ant walks near, the doodlebug reaches out and grabs it in its jaws. The ant is then dragged down to the bottom of the hole and eaten.

In spite of their many enemies, ants flourish in almost every part of the world. They are among the most interesting of all insects, and the habits of many of them often surprise us. Fossil ants have been found that are estimated to have lived more than a hundred million years ago. Ants have lived on the earth far longer than man.